Short Stories for Students, Volume 12

Staff

Editor: Jennifer Smith.

Contributing Editors: Anne Marie Hacht, Michael L. LaBlanc, Ira Mark Milne, Elizabeth Thomason.

Managing Editor, Literature Content: Dwayne D. Hayes.

Managing Editor, Literature Product: David Galens.

Publisher, Literature Product: Mark Scott.

Content Capture: Joyce Nakamura, *Managing Editor*.Michelle Poole, *Associate Editor*.

Research: Victoria B. Cariappa, *Research Manager*.Cheryl Warnock, *Research Specialist*.Tamara Nott, Trade A. Richardson, *Research Associates*.Nicodemus Ford, Sarah Genik, Timothy Lehnerer, Ron Morelli, *Research Assistants*.

Permissions: Maria Franklin, *Permissions Manager*. Jacqueline Jones, Julie Juengling, *Permissions Assistants*.

Manufacturing: Mary Beth Trimper, *Manager, Composition and Electronic Prepress*.Evi Seoud, *Assistant Manager, Composition Purchasing and Electronic Prepress*.Stacy Melson, *Buyer*.

Imaging and Multimedia Content Team: Barbara Yarrow, *Manager*.Randy Bassett, *Imaging Supervisor*.Robert Duncan, Dan Newell, *Imaging Specialists*.Pamela A. Reed, *Imaging Coordinator* .Leitha Etheridge-Sims, Mary Grimes, David G. Oblender, *Image Catalogers*.Robyn V. Young, *Project Manager*.Dean Dauphinais, *Senior Image Editor*. Kelly A. Quin, *Image Editor*.

Product Design Team: Kenn Zorn, *Product Design Manager*.Pamela A. E. Galbreath, *Senior Art Director*.Michael Logusz, *Graphic Artist*.

The Gale Group
27500 Drake Road
Farmington Hills, MI 48331-3535

ISBN 0-7876-4264-9
ISSN 1092-7735

Printed in the United States of America.
10 9 8 7 6 5 4 3 2 1

Heart of Darkness

Joseph Conrad

1899

Introduction

Joseph Conrad's long short story, "Heart of Darkness" (1899), is considered to be his greatest literary achievement, as well as his most controversial. It was first published in *Blackwood's Magazine* in 1899, in three monthly installments. In 1902, it was republished in a book entitled *Youth: A Narrative, and Two Other Stories*.

The story is partly based on Conrad's personal experiences as the captain of a riverboat on the Congo River, and was immediately interpreted as an indictment of the colonial rule of the Belgian government in the Congo. The story is characterized by a narrative embedded in a narrative; the "frame" narrator relates a story told him by the sailor Charlie Marlow, Conrad's famous character who appears as a storyteller in much of his fiction. Marlow relates his experiences as the captain of a steamboat, sent down the Congo River in the employ of an unnamed ivory company, to retrieve Kurtz, a company manager whose "methods" had become "unsound."

The central symbolism of the "heart of darkness" has been interpreted in several ways. On one level, it represents the "darkness" at the "heart" of men's souls—the descent into an evil that lurks in the hearts of all men. In this sense, it is a psychological journey into the unconscious. On a somewhat more literal level, the journey represents a descent into the "darkness" or evil of imperialism—the greed for ivory and other resources that characterized the exploitation of African people by European colonialism. African writer Chinua Achebe has interpreted the story's central symbolism in terms of a racist perception of Africa and African people as representative of more "primitive" or "savage," less evolved society, representing the repressed desires of European society. Achebe interprets Conrad's story in these terms as thoroughly racist. Other critics have countered Achebe's interpretation in terms that defend Conrad as a critic of racist imperialism.

Author Biography

Novelist and short story writer Joseph Conrad was born Jozef Teodor Konrad Korzeniowski on December 3, 1857, in Berdiczew, Podolia, then part of the Russian Empire (now Poland). His father, Apollo Nalecz Korzeniowski, was a resistance organizer against Russian rule in Poland; in 1861, he was arrested for these activities, and sentenced to exile in Vologda in northern Russia, accompanied by his wife and son. Conrad's mother, whose tuberculosis was worsened by the harsh weather, died in 1865, when Conrad was eight years old.

At this time, Conrad was introduced to literature and to the English language by his father, a poet and translator. In 1869, his father died, also of tuberculosis. Conrad was left in the care of relatives, eventually under the guardianship of his uncle, Tadeusz Bobrowski, a lawyer, who supported and encouraged Conrad financially, professionally, and emotionally, throughout his life.

Yearning from an early age to be a sailor, Conrad went to Marseilles in 1874, and eventually served for sixteen years in the British merchant navy. In 1886, he became a British citizen, and earned a master mariner's certificate. In 1889, he had the opportunity to command a Congo river boat, realizing a childhood dream of going to Africa. His most famous and most critically acclaimed story, "Heart of Darkness," was based on his experiences in Africa.

In 1894, his beloved uncle died. By this time, Conrad had retired from sea travel and settled in England, becoming a full-time writer. His first novel, *Almayer's Folly,* was published in 1895 under the newly assumed name, Joseph Conrad. Also in 1895, at the age of thirty-eight, he married twenty-two-year old Jessie George, with whom he had two sons. His second novel, *An Outcast of the Islands,* was published in 1896.

Conrad became known as a novelist of sea adventures, but his literary style and thematic concerns as expressed through these stories were of a more serious nature. Among his works which take place at sea are *The Nigger of the "Narcissus"*(1897), *Lord Jim*(1900), *Youth*(1902), and *Typhoon*(1902). He died of a heart attack on August 3, 1924.

Plot Summary

“Heart of Darkness” begins with the “frame” narrator’s description of a group of men relaxing on a private yacht one evening. One of the men, Charlie Marlow, a sailor, commences to tell his friends a tale of one of his adventures as the captain of a steamboat going down the Congo River. The rest of the narrative consists of Marlow’s tale, with only occasional interruptions by the “frame” narrator to describe Marlow and his storytelling style.

Marlow’s tale is about his assignment to work for “the Company,” an ivory trading company in what was then the Free State of the Congo, a colony of the Belgian government. Marlow is assigned to retrieve a certain Kurtz, a company manager operating deep in the Congo to retrieve ivory whose “methods” were reported to be “unsound.” Marlow initially stops at one of the Company sites, where he is appalled by the brutal, inhumane, slavery-like conditions of the African people made to work for the Company. He comes upon a grove where those who have been worked nearly to starvation and death lie in wait for death. Marlow is equally appalled, although ironically impressed, with the callousness of the company management and bureaucracy toward the suffering Africans. Making several stops at company sites, Marlow hears intriguing reference to the enigmatic Kurtz, to the point that he himself becomes eager to meet and converse with the man.

As Marlow's boat moves closer to Kurtz's compound, the small steamboat crew are barraged with deadly arrows, even as they are blinded by a thick fog. Marlow watches in sympathy as one of the Africans on his boat dies from an arrow wound. He is struck by his sense of identification with the black man. Arriving at Kurtz's compound, Marlow meets with a man he refers to as the Russian Harlequin soldier, who maniacally and obsessively worships Kurtz. Marlow observes decapitated human heads stuck on poles throughout the compound. He then finds Kurtz himself, a shriveled up man dying of malarial fever. As he takes the dying Kurtz aboard his boat, Marlow observes a woman who seems to have been Kurtz's companion, mourning his departure. As they make their way back up the river, Kurtz soon dies, with the enigmatic and haunting words "The horror! The horror!" on his lips. Marlow is then taken up with fever and illness, which renders him delirious. Upon recovering, Marlow returns to England, where he goes to visit Kurtz's "Intended," the woman Kurtz was engaged to marry. Marlow has come to give her the packet of letters and writings Kurtz had entrusted with him. Although he abhors liars and lying, Marlow withholds from her Kurtz's haunting final words, telling her instead that he had died with her own name on his lips.

Characters

The Harlequin Russian Soldier

The Harlequin Russian soldier greets Marlow upon his arrival at Kurtz's compound. A Westerner, he seems half-crazed and maniacally obsessed with the worship of Kurtz as an exceptional being.

Kurtz

Kurtz is a Company employee of "unsound methods," whom Marlow has been charged with retrieving from the depths of the Congo. Marlow becomes increasingly intrigued by the enigmatic Kurtz, eventually craving above all else to converse with him. What Marlow finds at the end of his journey is a man dying of malaria. However, it becomes clear that Kurtz has become an object of some dread and worship among the local inhabitants, and that his ruthless "methods" of obtaining vast quantities of ivory have become brutal and inhumane. Kurtz represents the greed and cruelty of the imperialist exploitation of the Congo by the Belgian government that had colonized it.

Kurtz's Intended

Upon his death, Kurtz refers to his "Intended," his fiancee, a white woman living in London. At the end of the story, Marlow goes to visit her in her lavish home. The story ends with Marlow's lie, that Kurtz had died with her name upon his lips. There is some sense that she knows Marlow is lying.

Charlie Marlow

Marlow is the narrator of the central"framed" narrative of the story. The character of Marlow appears in a number of Conrad's stories, often in the role of observer and narrator of the central events of the story. Marlow is a sailor whose narrative relates his experiences under hire by an unnamed ivory company to take a riverboat down the Congo River in order to retrieve Kurtz, a maverick company manager. Marlow is appalled at the treatment of the African people by the Company; but he is also disturbed by the behavior of the Africans, which seem to him "mysterious." Marlow eventually finds Kurtz, who is dying of malaria, and brings him aboard the steamboat. Kurtz dies shortly thereafter, and then Marlow himself is stricken with fever and illness. When he returns to England, he visits Kurtz's "Intended," his fiancee, to give her some of Kurtz's personal writings. Although Kurtz's enigmatic dying words were "The horror! The horror!" Marlow, who abhors liars, himself lies to the Intended, telling her that Kurtz's final words had been her name. Marlow's perspective on what he witnesses in the Congo is somewhat ambivalent, and is the source of much critical debate among literary scholars, particularly in terms of his perspective on the African people; the matter of whether or not Marlow's, or Conrad's, perspective is racist has been argued persuasively on both sides, and is a subject of ongoing debate.

Media Adaptations

- The 1978 movie *Apocalypse Now,* directed by Francis Ford Coppola, is adapted from Conrad's "Heart of Darkness." The film is set during the Vietnam War. Martin Sheen plays Captain Willard, a stand-in for Conrad's narrator Charlie Marlow; Kurtz is played by Marlon Brando. There was a 1994 adaptation directed by Nicolas Roeg and starring John Malkovich as Kurtz and Tim Roth as Marlowe.

The Narrator

The narrator of the story is a character only insofar as he relates to the reader a story told him by Marlow. He is therefore referred to as the "frame narrator," because his narrative merely frames the central narrative, which is related by Marlow. For this reason, most of the seventy-five page story is written as a direct quotation from Marlow. The frame narrator only occasionally pauses to describe Marlow's character and the small group of men listening to his story.

Themes

Civilization and the Primitive

The central theme around which this story revolves is civilization versus wilderness. The symbolism that represents this theme is the opposition of light versus darkness. As in much of European art and literature, the imagery of "light" is associated with Western culture, civilization, knowledge, and the conscious mind. The imagery of"darkness," on the other hand, is associated with Third World cultures (such as Africa), the "primitive" or "savage," the unknown or mysterious, and the psychological unconscious. Many of the themes in Conrad's story are based on this set of oppositions. Thus, European culture is contrasted with African culture, where African culture is seen to represent the primitive, unconscious mind of the white European man. Marlow's narrative of his journey down the Congo River, and his encounter with Kurtz, expresses the anxiety of the white man who is tempted by his foray into the "wilderness" to "go native," lose the trappings of civilization, and revert to a more "primitive" state of mind. As writer Chinua Achebe has pointed out, this conceptual construct on the part of Western cultures in their perceptions and representations of African culture is thoroughly racist. Other critics have argued, however, that Conrad's story is a critique of the racist colonial mentality of the Europeans in Africa.

Capitalist Exploitation

Conrad's story is critical of the "methods" of the white European "Company" that, motivated by pure greed, exploits African resources and labor. Conrad's commentary is in part based on his own experiences with the ivory business in the Congo, and is supported by historical records that make it clear that the ivory trade in Africa was brutal on a par with the slave trade. Conrad mocks such European trade practices through his ironic representation of the generically named "Company," which clearly stands in for the presence of European companies in Africa. The Company management is also portrayed ironically, such as the manager who maintains a high starched white collar in spite of the signs of suffering and cruelty that he perpetuates in the treatment of the Africans. Conrad also satirizes the values of "efficiency" practiced by the Company as both irrational and inhumane. The character of Kurtz, whose "methods" are "unsound," represents the height of hypocrisy—the "methods" of the Company seem to be thoroughly "unsound," from a moral perspective.

Topics for Further Study

- The movie *Apocalypse Now,* directed by Francis Ford Coppola, is based on Conrad's "Heart of Darkness." Compare and contrast it to Conrad's story. What elements of the original story are preserved in the film? Conrad's story is a commentary on the conditions of imperialism in the Congo in the late nineteenth century; Coppola's film is a commentary on the involvement of the United States in the Vietnam War. What, in your opinion, makes Conrad's story appropriate to the situation of the Vietnam War? How would you describe Coppola's vision of the Vietnam war, and what perspective does he present? In what ways is the character of Kurtz different in the story and in the movie?

- Writer Chinua Achebe has criticized Conrad's "Heart of Darkness" as a racist depiction of Africa. Achebe's well-known novel, *Things Fall Apart,* is a very different representation of Africa, in what ways are Africa and Africans depicted differently in Achebe's novel as compared to Conrad's story?
- "Heart of Darkness" is based on Conrad's experiences in the Congo in the 1890s. Learn more about the history of the Congo in the nineteenth and twentieth centuries. What social, political, and economic changes has it gone through during the century since Conrad's story was published?
- Conrad's father was a resistance organizer in the Polish rebellion against the rule of the Russian empire in the nineteenth century. Learn more about the history of Poland under the Russian empire. What are the major events, and changes in Poland over the past century?
- Conrad's novel *Lord Jim,* another sea story, was adapted to the screen

in a 1965 film directed by Richard Brooks, and starring Peter O'Toole and James Mason. What themes does it address? In what ways is the story concerned with similar elements of human nature and character to those in "Heart of Darkness?" What elements of story does the film provide that are not possible in the written medium of the novel?

Race and Racism

Whether or not one concludes that Conrad's story is racist, it is clear that the issue of race and racism in the European colonies is a central theme of the story. Marlow links colonial conquest directly to racism in the often-quoted passage: "The conquest of the earth, which mostly means the taking it away from those who have a different complexion or slightly flatter noses than ourselves, is not a pretty thing when you look into it too much." At the same time, however, the modern reader is struck by Conrad's nonchalant use of the term "nigger," which is now considered thoroughly racist.

Lies

Marlow's narrative includes an underlying

theme regarding lies and lying. Marlow explains to his listeners his disdain for lies and lying:

> There is a taint of death, a flavour of mortality in lies—which is exactly what I hate and detest in the world—what I want to forget. It makes me miserable and sick like biting something rotten would do.

And yet, when faced with Kurtz's"Intended," at the end of the story, Marlow deliberately defies his own values in choosing to lie to her about Kurtz's final words. Unable to bring himself to do "justice" to Kurtz's dying wish that he be properly represented, Marlow refrains from repeating those haunting words, "The horror! The horror!" telling her instead that Kurtz had died with her name on his lips. Feeling that he has sinned in telling this lie, Marlow half expects "that the heavens would fall upon my head," but concludes that"the heavens do not fall for such a trifle." Aware that he has betrayed Kurtz through his lie, Marlow's justification seems to be a desire to protect the white woman from the truth of the true evil that lurks in the soul of man: "I could not tell her. It would have been too dark—too dark altogether."

Style

Narration

Narrative technique is an important element of Conrad's literary style. This story is structured as an "embedded narrative." This means that the central story, narrated by the fictional character Charlie Marlow, is "embedded" in a "frame" narrative, whereby the "frame" narrator introduces Marlow's character, and presents the central story as a direct quotation from Marlow. For this reason, nearly every paragraph of the story begins with a quotation mark, indicating that it is a continuation of the frame narrator's direct quotation of Marlow's narration. This type of "embedded" narrative constitutes the structure of several of Conrad's stories, as the character of Marlow is the "embedded" narrator. This narrative structure focuses the reader's attention as much on the art of storytelling, and the character of the storyteller, as it does on the central story itself. Conrad's "frame" narrator calls attention to the significance of the frame narrator in describing Marlow's storytelling style. The narrator uses the metaphor of a "nut"—indicating that, for Marlow, the meaning of the story lies more in the "shell" (the narration) than in the "nut" (the central story) it contains:

> The yarns of seamen have a direct simplicity, the whole meaning of

> which lies within the shell of a cracked nut. But Marlow was not typical (if his propensity to spin yarns be excepted) and to him the meaning of an episode was not inside like a kernel but outside, enveloping the tale which brought it out only as a glow brings out a haze, in the likeness of one of these misty halos that, sometimes, are made visible by the spectral illumination of moonshine.

Setting

The setting of the frame narrative is in England, as a group of men relax on a private yacht. The central story, narrated by the sailor Marlow, takes place on the Congo River, in an area of Africa then colonized by the Belgian King Leopold II, who deceptively named it the Free State of the Congo. The story takes place in the 1890s. The setting is significant because the tale is based in part on Conrad's own personal experiences as the captain of a riverboat on the Congo in the 1890s. Conrad's character of Marlow relates the brutal, slave-like conditions under which the native Africans were treated by their Belgian colonizers, and the story was interpreted upon initial publication in 1899 as an indictment of Belgian imperialism. The ivory company for which Marlow works represents the historical circumstances of the ivory trade in Africa, by which European colonizers greedily exploited both the African people for their labor and the resources of the continent. Conrad paints an unflattering picture of the European presence in Africa during the colonial period.

Imagery: Light and Darkness

The central imagery of the story revolves around the binary oppositions suggested in the title: light and darkness. This imagery sets up a contrast between the "light" white Europeans in Africa, and the "dark" native Africans. Likewise, the "light" is suggestive of European "civilization," while the "darkness" refers to the culture of the African people, which Europeans perceived as "primitive" and "savage." The imagery of light and darkness also refers metaphorically to the "light" of what is now referred to as the "conscious" self, which the Europeans associated with their own society, as opposed to the "darkness" of the unconscious, which the Europeans associated with African society. The "light" also represents the realm of that which is known and understandable to the Europeans (their own culture and native land), as opposed to the unknown (darkness), "mysterious" land, peoples and cultures of the African continent. How one interprets the story generally revolves around this central axis of light/dark imagery, and the variety of metaphorical and symbolic implications of this imagery.

Historical Context

Apocalypse Now

The 1978 film *Apocalypse Now,* directed by Francis Ford Coppola, is based on Conrad's story "Heart of Darkness." While Conrad's story is set in the Congo in the 1890s, and is a commentary on imperialism in the form of Belgian colonization, Coppola's film is set during the Vietnam War in the 1960s, and is a commentary on U.S. involvement in the Vietnam conflict. Coppola retained the central narrative trajectory, in which a Captain Willard (played by Martin Sheen), substituted for Conrad's character Marlow, is sent on a mission to retrieve a renegade Colonel Kurtz (played by Marlon Brando), whose"unsound methods" in Cambodia have caused alarm among military leaders. *Apocalypse Now* includes a notable performance by Dennis Hopper as the character equivalent to Conrad's Harlequin Russian soldier, who maniacally worships Kurtz. While critics agree that Coppola's film is an impressive achievement in cinematic style, they disagree on the political implications of the film. It is clearly an indictment of U.S. involvement in Vietnam, but is full of ambiguity in its greater implications. The documentary, *Hearts of Darkness*(1992), chronicles the making of the film.

Compare & Contrast

- **Nineteenth Century:** The deceptively named Free State of the Congo is under the rule of the Belgian King Leopold II, who exploits the natural resources of the region, as well as its people in slavery-like conditions.

  Twentieth Century: The Free State of the Congo is renamed the Belgian Congo in 1908. It wins its independence from Belgium in 1960, and in 1965 Mobutu becomes president, renaming the nation Zaire in 1971. In 1997, Zaire is renamed the Democratic Republic of the Congo.

- **Nineteenth Century:** Under the rule of France and Holland before 1830, Belgium attains national independence in 1831 through the Belgian Revolution. In 1831, King Leopold I becomes the first king of the newly established nation. On his death in 1865 he is succeeded by his son, Leopold II, who rules until his own death in 1909.

  Twentieth Century: Leopold II is succeeded by his nephew King Albert I, who rules from 1909 to 1934. From 1914 to 1918, during the first World War, Belgium is occupied by Germany. When national independence in the years following World War I. During World War II, Poland is occupied by Nazi Germany and Russia, and after the war it comes under Communist control. With the 1989 collapse of communism in Eastern Europe, Poland begins the process of converting to a democratic government with a free-market economy.

The Congo

"Heart of Darkness" is based on Conrad's experiences as the captain of a steamboat in the Congo River (the second longest river in Africa, after the Nile) during the 1890s. At that time, the Congo was under the rule of King Leopold II of Belgium. Although he "gave" what was then called The Free State of the Congo to the Belgian people in 1895, his rule over the region effectively remained until his death in 1909. Under Leopold's rule, the African people were exploited for their work, and treated as badly and brutally as slaves. Upon Leopold's death, it became the Belgian Congo, and was ruled by Belgium until 1960, when it won independence. Between 1960 and 1965, the region suffered from the political upheaval of formulating a new government. In 1965, Joseph-Desire Mobutu became president of the Congo. In

Belgium is liberated from the Germans and the king is restored to power in 1918, universal male suffrage (for those over age 21) is instituted (women do not get the right to vote in Belgium until 1948). In 1934, King Leopold III succeeds his father Albert. In 1940, during World War II, Belgium is once again invaded and occupied by Germany. After refusing to flee the country, King Leopold III is held prisoner by the Germans until 1945. In 1951, Leopold III abdicates in favor of his son, Baudouin, who reigns until 1993. Between 1971 and 1992, Belgium goes through the process of becoming a federal state made up of several autonomous regions, including the Flemish region, the Walloon region, and Brussels. In 1993, the second son of Leopold III, now Albert II, succeeds to the throne.

- **Nineteenth Century:** During Conrad's lifetime, his native Poland is under the rule of the Russian Empire. Conrad's father is a member of a resistance organization, which fights unsuccessfully for Polish independence from Russia.

  Twentieth Century: Poland gains

1971, Mobutu changed the country's name to Zaire, and his own name to Mobutu Sese Seko, as well as changing the names of other places within the nation. In 1997, it became the Democratic Republic of the Congo.

Ford Madox Ford

Conrad became a personal friend and co-author of the novelist Ford Madox Ford, with whom he wrote two books. Ford, considered among the greatest of novelists, is best known for *The Good Soldier*(1915). Other important works include *Parade's End,* a four-part series made up of: *Some Do Not*(1924), *No More Parades*(1925), *A Man Could Stand Up*(1926), and *Last Post*(1928). Ford was known for his close association with many of the great writers of his day, and for his encouragement of younger writers.

Blackwood's Magazine

"Heart of Darkness" was first published in three monthly installment's in *Blackwood's Magazine. Blackwood's Magazine* was an important literary influence in nineteenth-century Britain. It was originally founded by William Blackwood, a Scottish bookseller, in 1817, originally entitled *Edinburgh Monthly Magazine,* and later *Blackwood's Edinburgh Magazine;* in 1905 it became *Blackwood's Magazine.*Originally focusing on political satire, it was also a literary journal publishing poems, short stories, and novels in serial form. Eventually, it became less political and more literary, publishing works of such renowned authors as George Eliot and Anthony Trollope as well as Joseph Conrad.

Critical Overview

"Heart of Darkness" is widely considered to be Conrad's masterpiece. It was first published in *Blackwood's Magazine* in a series of three installments, in February, March, and April of 1899. In 1902, it was published in the book, *Youth: A Narrative, and Two Other Stories.*

"Heart of Darkness" was understood by critics at the time of its initial publication as an indictment of Belgian colonial rule in the Free State of the Congo (now the Democratic Republic of the Congo). According to Robert F. Haugh, in *Joseph Conrad,* "The story was taken by some as an attack upon Belgian colonial methods in the Congo; as a moral tract; and as a study of race relationships." Haugh goes on to say that, "Most contemporary reviewers read it as a criticism of Belgian colonialism, an issue that remained alive until Conrad's death and got attention in his obituary notices." Other reviewers interpreted the story in terms of Christian religious iconography. As Haugh explains, "Paul Wiley, in his *Conrad's Measure of Man* ...finds the myth of the fall from innocence throughout Conrad, and ... makes of Kurtz the man driven from the Garden of Eden."

More recent critical debate on "Heart of Darkness" has focused on the issue of whether the story is actually a critique of racism, or if the story is based on a fundamentally racist perspective. In a lecture first given in 1975, entitled "An Image of Africa," African novelist Chinua Achebe made the argument that, based on this story, "Joseph Conrad was a thoroughgoing racist." Achebe argues that the story is structured on a common racist conception in Western thought, which perceives African people as uncivilized and white people as civilized, and that Conrad, rather than challenging racist conceptions, "chose the role of purveyor of comforting myths. 'Heart of Darkness' projects the image of Africa as 'the other world,' the antithesis of Europe and therefore of civilization, a place where man's vaunted intelligence and refinement are finally mocked by triumphant bestiality." Achebe goes on to explain that this story continues the racist conception that conceives"Africa as setting and backdrop which eliminates the African as human factor. Africa as a metaphysical battlefield devoid of all recognizable humanity. ..." Achebe goes on to criticize the body of Western criticism of Conrad's story, which continues to overlook these racist assumptions."That this simple truth is glossed over in criticisms of his work is due to the fact that white racism against Africa is such a normal way of thinking that its manifestations go completely unremarked." Achebe posits that "the question is whether a novel which celebrates this dehumanization, which depersonalizes a portion of the human race, can be called a great work of art. My answer is: No, it cannot." He concludes that Conrad's "obvious racism has, however, not been addressed. And it is high time it was!"

Francis B. Singh, in a 1978 essay entitled "The

Colonialistic Bias of 'Heart of Darkness,'" on the other hand, states that "it is a truth universally acknowledged that 'Heart of Darkness' is one of the most powerful indictments of colonialism ever written." He qualifies this statement, however, by concluding that "ambivalent, in fact, is probably the most accurate way to sum up Conrad's attitude toward colonialism." Singh goes on to explain that "the compromises that Marlow makes, as when he fights off identification with the blacks or when he tells lies about Kurtz to prevent the civilized Western world from collapsing, stem from Conrad's own inability to face unflinchingly the nature of colonialism." C. P. Saravan, in a 1980 article entitled "Racism and the 'Heart of Darkness,'" makes the claim that Conrad was not necessarily in agreement with his fictional character of Marlow on his perceptions of Africa and Africans. Saravan claims that "it is not correct to say that Marlow has Conrad's complete confidence," and that the "ironic distance between Marlow and Conrad should not be overlooked." He asserts that, through this story, "Conrad suggests that Europe's claim to be civilized and therefore superior, needs earnest reexamination." Saravan concludes that "Conrad was not entirely immune to the infection of the beliefs and attitudes of his age, but he was ahead of most in trying to break free."

Sources

Achebe, Chinua, "An Image of Africa: Racism in Conrad's 'Heart of Darkness,'" in *Heart of Darkness,* 3d ed., Norton, 1988, pp. 251–53, 256–59.

Haugh, Robert F., '"Heart of Darkness': Problem for Critics," in *Heart of Darkness,* 3d ed., Norton, 1988, pp. 239,241.

Saravan, C. P., "Racism and the 'Heart of Darkness,'" in *Heart of Darkness,* 3d ed., Norton, 1988, pp. 282, 283, 285.

Singh, Frances B., "The Colonialistic Bias of 'Heart of Darkness,'" in *Heart of Darkness,* 3d ed., Norton, 1988, pp. 268, 269, 279.

Further Reading

Batchelor, John, *The Life of Joseph Conrad: A Critical Biography,* Blackwell, 1994.

> Batchelor's book is a recent biography of Conrad, published by Blackwell press, which originally published many of Conrad's stories and novels.

Hammer, Robert D., ed., *Joseph Conrad: Third World Perspectives,* Three Continents Press, 1990.

> Conrad has been criticized for his Eurocentric depictions of Africa and other "Third World" cultures; this collection of critical essays presents a variety of Third World perspectives on Conrad's work.

Hochschild, Adam, *King Leopold's Ghost: A Story of Greed, Terror, and Heroism in Colonial Africa,* Houghton Mifflin, 1998.

> This work is a history of Colonial Africa under Belgian King Leopold II, during the period in which several of Conrad's stories take place.

Moore, Gene M., ed., *Conrad on Film,* Cambridge University Press, 1997.

> Moore's collection of critical essays on film adaptations of Conrad stories

includes several essays on *Apocalypse Now,* which was based on "Heart of Darkness."

Nelson, Samuel H., *Colonialism in the Congo Basin, 1880–1940,* Ohio University Center for International Studies, 1994.

This work is a history of European conquest and colonization of the Congo during the period in which several of Conrad's stories take place.

Roberts, Andrew Michael, ed., *Conrad and Gender,* Rodopi, 1993.

This text is a collection of critical essays on Conrad's representations of sex, gender, and sexuality in his fictional work.

Wilson, Derek, and Peter Ayerst, *White Gold: The Story of African Ivory,* Heinemann, 1976.

Wilson's and Ayerst's book provides a history of the ivory trade in Africa.

www.ingramcontent.com/pod-product-compliance
Lightning Source LLC
Chambersburg PA
CBHW050835201224
19286CB00005B/113